*for MARY ANNE SIOK, best friend,
secret keeper, sister...my person*

WAITING OUT THE STORM

JENNIFER A. PAYNE

THREE CHAIRS PUBLISHING
BRANFORD, CONNECTICUT - 2022

© 2019, 2022, Jennifer A. Payne

All rights reserved. Please respect the copyright of this book — its contents reflect hours of creative effort, predawn conversations with muses, and hundreds of pots of coffee. We ask that you do not reproduce or translate this in any form or by any means, digital, electronic, or mechanical, including photocopying, recording, or by any information storage and retrieval system, without permission in writing or by email from the publisher, except for the use of brief quotations in a book review or related article. Thank you!

Cover Art: Crow, Esther Elzinga of StudioTokek, hand carved rubber stamp, www.etsy.com/shop/StudioTokek.

Book Design by Words by Jen (Branford, CT)
Printed in the U.S.A.

ISBN: 978-0-9905651-4-7

POETRY / Death, Grief, Loss / Nature

Three Chairs Publishing
P.O. Box 453
Branford, CT 06405

www.3chairspublishing.com

"Not till we are lost, in other words not till
we have lost the world, do we begin to find
ourselves, and realize where we are
and the infinite extent of our relations."

— Henry David Thoreau

"Through the empty branches the sky remains.
It is what you have.
Be earth now, and evensong.
Be the ground lying under that sky."

— Rainer Maria Rilke

POEMS

there but for the grace of god	7
extant	8
the contemplative life	9
sky burial	10
at the passing	11
if i could talk to the animals…	12
on the likelihood of bears and change	13
the missing	14
i'm sorry for your loss	15
and they will carry her soul to heaven	16
resilience plan	17
walking destiny's fine line	18
a tour of grief	19
shape-shifter time-shifter crow	20
this bridge	21
she is walking, spent	22
prayer	24
at race point beach	25
waiting out the storm in room 217	26
horseshoe crabs on the morning-after beach	27
you, after life	28
a passing glance	29
hoping for magic: a found poem	30
she reminds me	31
estuary	32
gratitude	33
on the discovery of an owl pellet by a poet	34

there but for the grace of god

you don't need
technology's tap - tap - tap
to tell you a storm's coming

from this south-facing beach
the sidewinder waves
are forecast enough

a pockmarked sand
spares little for grounded gull
or me, here and searching

the whites of brants and buffleheads
flash distress along the surf
or just fair warning   I cannot tell

one soul, solo
floats an unseen current
too far out to save

this is no fit place to be alone
my prayer for it and me
in wind, whorled away

extant

The nautilus shell
is complicated.

Mathematical —
its presentation
logarithmic,
mirror of the
greatest storms,
the largest galaxies…

Its whole wide whorl
compartmentalized
with past lives
in secret chambers —
where poetry is found
no less.

The poetry of time,
this old soul,
reminder of
roots and bones,
our beginnings
and our end.

the contemplative life

The contemplative life
of the kitchen spider
was extinguished
by the uninvited
cellar spider
on the eve of the
blue moon full moon
yet neither made a sound.

The spider —
in the unexpected face
of its own demise
was silent.

The moon —
in its rare and wild
traverse across heaven —
was silent, too.

Yet my mind chattered endless —
what small worries creep?
what large burdens travel?
what of death? and heaven?

This contemplative life
aches for the enviable silence.

sky burial

This morning she was blood red,
so freshly gone, I thought I saw
the last breath, her spirit leave,
but it was only a breeze
whispering to the underside
of her soft furred belly.

Now she is curbside,
brown and gone —
curled up fetal and food
for flies and birds,
this her sky burial,
memory aloft and scattered.

Promise me this…
that if we come back
you will make sure I return
in as many places as possible:
the field and the fen,
the hollow of pine on the back bend,
that long wide beach of Nauset.

at the passing

Clearly dropped
and otherwise,
the remains of what was
draped backwards
on a branch
in the misty
morning woods,
nothing spared
for crow
but bones.
Macabre perhaps
but fascinating
enough for us
to step deep
into the thicket
for a closer look,
a prayer of passing,
and conjecture
at the what and how
it came to be there.
Wonder at the mysteries
we will never solve —
how its life force left
and indeed
how might ours?

if i could talk to the animals…

The spotted salamander
— one —
on an incline, dying
cradled and
tucked under leaves
for safe keeping
then
— two —
an old red fox,
lame and confused,
shepherded
patiently
off the road,
and
— three —
prehistoric titan
this turtle trapped
near a long fence
of iron and wire
— and me —
with a stick
this way, this way
like a kinder, gentler
St. Patrick
wondering
did Noah ever weep?

on the likelihood of bears and change

I am watching for bears this morning
out the wide window of a friend
who insists there are bears
in the woods I watch.

But watching for bears — waiting –
is a futile pursuit, as bears
will come and go at their leisure
neither here nor there at your reckoning.

Neither here nor there but where and when they please —
bears — you can wait and worry all you like
but when the bear is ready to reveal itself
only then does it appear, and only then should you worry.

Only then should you worry — wonder:
should I lie down and make for dead
or be brave in the face of all that I fear?
Only then. Wonder.

the missing

At 3 a.m., it is hard to tell
conversation from dream:
was that you   laughing
or just the memory of?
If I cover my head
to hide the revealing moon,
can we pick back up again?
Talk about whatever,
smile in that easy, easy way,
share our secrets and laugh
without reservation…
or would you remain shadow,
ever crossing my path like this,
without regard for the missing?

i'm sorry for your loss

There is a distinct silence to grief,
as if a million stars —
the fallen and collapsing —
catch in the throat,
a swarming cosmic mass
that quiets the unspoken,
unfinished,
and unanswered.
There, swirling, all of the light   gone
Nothing but stale words stuck
to the roof of your mouth,
trite and of no use to any poet
she, wondering, *Why speak at all?*

and they will carry her soul to heaven

she is blue light,

the color of sky,

the fork-tailed bird

who flies unexpected

ever dancing with

swoops and swirls,

the song on the radio,

a familiar beat

for a silent heart

soaring in the blue,

with a flutter

and a wave

and a shimmy shake,

I am sure of it.

resilience plan

It was supposed to be
the two of us —
forces of nature
against the winds,
sheltered in place
with the stories
only we remembered,
(or didn't anymore).
That was the contingency
if all else failed —
if our tethered moorings
proved futile against the currents.
We would make room
and accommodations,
adaptations we never mentioned,
save for who would get the couch
and who the chair where the cat slept,
who would pick the dance music,
and who would cook the roast chicken.
We hadn't prepared for
a sudden erosion of familiar,
this unpredictable path
in a deep, cold surge of loss.

walking destiny's fine line

We didn't mention it that day,
the odd drag of the left foot
its sound like an after-thought…

second thoughts now
and too much time passed
to make a difference.

She never listened anyway
and who was I to
preach or teach or cajole?

We each bear our own weight
carry with us the things
we can't put down

and after a while they break us
prove too much for this fragile vessel
that bursts into a thousand stars.

Our destiny is all of that, right there,
following us around with an odd echo drag
few of us ever, ever mention.

a tour of grief

*"Orca Mother Drops Calf After Unprecedented
17 Days of Mourning" - National Geographic*

Did the whale think:
What if he dies *today*?
He, her companion,
or elder, or child.
What if he dies today?
Did she compensate
ahead of time for the loss
with more love than one
could pour into an ocean...
or was she as careless as us,
our heavy heads
so full of nonsense —
too preoccupied to consider
What if he dies today?
Could she stop time,
touch the moment, there:
    I loved you
    I love you
    I will always love you
before time cast her adrift
left to carry her grief
across the vast and endless
sea ahead.

shape-shifter time-shifter crow

Like a song from then
and there
the crow calls from a tree
outside the tap - tap - tap
of my office day
and I am transported
to tranquil mornings by the shore,
to waves rolling and gulls
those parking lot gossips
who don't mind my mood,
my unkempt hair,
my long tale of grief
that drags across the sand
gathering debris
and memories
to repurpose into poems
someday

someday
soon
the gulls remind
the crow reminds
and I almost

almost

remember how to breathe.

this bridge

Here is the coming
and the going,
the where we cross over.
Attraversiamo,
says the traveler,
Let's cross over.
Let's find a way
from this to that,
from here to there.
Move.
Change.
Navigate.
Negotiate.

Don't hesitate.

Let's cross over
this coming and going
crossover,
become again

what's next.

she is walking, spent

She is walking, spent

remembers: the recoverable wave energy resource
here is 160 terawatt hours per year

160 terawatt hours per year =
energy resource from ocean waves

enormous potential

consider: just 1 terawatt hour per year of energy
could supply 93,850 homes with power

could   potentially

if recoverable

can it be recovered?

While an abundance of wave energy is available, it cannot be fully harnessed everywhere for a variety of reasons...

One might need a Dragon to recover.

A large-scale effort

that reacts to pressure and stress

to generate power

the necessary power for 93,850 homes

or one

one person walking

walking by the waves one might harness

for energy resources

could   potentially

if recoverable

but is she?

prayer

If nothing,
grant me this:
this quiet walk
undisturbed
by anything
but winds and waves
but gulls and crows
but the long slow roll of the tide
and this
this welcomed solitude
the illusion of peace
and respite from memory
if nothing,
let that be enough
for now
amen.

at race point beach

whorls of wind   or ghosts
    howl at times
enough to steal a Banshee's wail   or mine

mine, loud and silent
this long, slow lament
undulating months and miles

months and miles to here,
where confessions of grief
keen to wind and waves

wind and waves wise enough
to hold me up

hold me up
a borrowed resolve
'til buffeted right again

again, moved   despite myself

waiting out the storm in room 217

The view is dim.
Hard to see what comes next
in a wicked, raging storm.

From this vantage point
weather vanes waver
north or south or both.

The wind blows back upon itself,
revisits old wounds,
its broken, battered past.

The waves lack such indecision,
storming the beach
relentless and determined

so that what remains is beaten down,
pieces of itself forever lost,
or holding on for dear, dear life.

horseshoe crabs on the morning-after beach

Molted self,
a variation discarded
on this wide expanse
of storm-washed beach,
where winds give and take
and waves give and take.

Am I the given or the taken?

How does one know
it's time to change,
make one's way
from this to that,
from here to there.
what is the calling that says
writhe out of these confines
wade back in — raw but ready —
shed of the old, naked and exposed
borne up by legs that move us
ever forward,
this blue ocean in our veins.

you, after life

It is always one bird   you
messenger, returning

the day you died
Sparrow flew quick!
to a branch nearby and I laughed
    you hated trees!

at the park that day
a Swallow,
patient and perched
with the missive
    I will always be with you

there have been others fleeting
or missed   like you

then here, a solitary Gull
in the haunted fog?

the lone Crow perched
outside the window

the Sanderling
stays a while
with me wading

like you did
in this place we loved

a passing glance

Hawk soars treetops
traveling southeast
to the Sound
then banks sharp-right
and west across the field,
from the corner of his eye
sees me precarious,
stopped at the road's fork,
me watching him
he watching me
cocks his head
curious for all the
moment I am due,
then slowly arcs
a wide curve home.

hoping for magic: a found poem

She wonders

What is the weight of a soul?

And

Where does it go when we die?

Asks in the dark

Are there such things as ghosts?
Can they speak to the living?

Please...

What of spirits, demons, fairies, and angels?
Can dreams hold portents, visions, foretellings?
Does magic exist?

say yes.

she reminds me

In the moment when
there is nothing left,
when hope has left
every small corner
and narrow path,
the Universe sets in —
reminds:

this wide-soaring Hawk

and brave, curious Deer,

a rare and precious Turtle,

the ancient Heron aloft,

a Bald Eagle perched,

this bold Barred Owl

remain.

estuary

this is where the tide meets the stream
where the salty brine of effort blends
into sweet and still relief, here
its transition imperceivable *almost*

how the churning changes
its temperament altered
there beneath the surface
wedged against itself

does it recognize its now and then
its before and after, each altered
forever, existing only here
and only in this moment —

it is the rare spirit who finds peace
in these wild moments of alteration

gratitude

For this
this ground beneath my feet
the signs of seasons, yes, and change
forever change

footsteps
   forward
      fortitude
fearlessness

solitude
communion

grace
   god

greatness in small things   and large
this, this ground beneath my feet

holds everything
   and me

spinning forward across a galaxy
   a universe

and She, of all things,
in every footstep

here, this ground beneath my feet

on the discovery of an owl pellet by a poet

This absurd amalgamation
of bone white memories,
what once was
now something
wholly other!

Holy other,
this reliquary of
god's creation,
every moving part —
what made it tick —
left here for time.

On bended knee,
the witness poet
should whisper
some ancient prayer
of gratitude.

Yes, gratitude...
for this is poetry incarnate,
the muscle and bone
of our experience,
how we ingest
and re-create.

How we take
what was...
make it new,
make it sacred

bone of my bones
and flesh of my flesh

ENDNOTES

Quote: *Walden*, Henry David Thoreau, (Boston and New York: Houghton Mifflin Company, 1854).

Quote: "Onto a Vast Plain," *Book of Hours: Love Poems to God*, Rainer Maria Rilke, Translated by Anita Barrows, Joanna Macy, (New York: Penguin, 2005).

EXTANT - The main feature of the Chambered Nautilus is its large coiled shell lined with mother-of-pearl. The shell is subdivided into as many as 30 chambers. As the shell grows, its body moves forward into the new larger chamber and produces a wall to seal off the older chambers. A cross-section of the Nautilus shell will show the cycles of its growth as a series of chambers arranged in a precise Golden Mean spiral, symbolic of life's unfolding mysteries. ("Sacred Geometry of the Nautilus Shell," 2muchfun.info/nautilusshell.html)

AND THEY WILL CARRY HER SOUL TO HEAVEN - The Swallow tattoo, depicting the fork-tailed bird, was a symbol used historically by sailors to show off their sailing experience. It is said that if the sailor drowns, the swallows will carry his soul to heaven. (Wikipedia)

A TOUR OF GRIEF - Inspired by the story of Tahlequah, see "Orca Mother Drops Calf, After Unprecedented 17 Days of Mourning," *National Geographic*, by Lori Cuthbert and Douglas Main (www.nationalgeographic.com, August 13, 2018).

SHAPE-SHIFTER TIME-SHIFTER CROW - Crow represents shapeshifting and mysticism. A shape-shifter is one that knows that this Earth walk is an illusion and that one can travel through space and time in the blink of an eye to appear in any form that is appropriate to bring help and healing to another. ("Crows & Ravens Carry Very Similar Medicine," Lynx Graywolf, morningstar.netfirms.com/crowmedicine.html).

SHE IS WALKING, SPENT - Statistics from the Bureau of Ocean Energy Management (www.boem.gov/Ocean-Wave-Energy/). A Dragon, or Wave Dragon, is a large-scale mechanism designed to generate electricity from ocean wave energy.

HORSESHOE CRABS ON THE MORNING-AFTER BEACH - Horseshoe Crabs, known for their blue-colored blood, grow through the process of molting their old shell, exiting out of the front segment of the old exoskeleton. They leave behind their entire exoskeleton—including its tail, legs, abdomen, gill coverings, eye coverings—which often wash ashore. (Massachusetts Division of Marine Fisheries)

HOPING FOR MAGIC: A FOUND POEM - Italicized text from *The Witches of New York*, Ami McKay (Harper Perennial, July 2017)

ESTUARY - Estuaries and their surrounding wetlands are bodies of water usually found where rivers meet the sea. They are home to unique plant and animal communities that have adapted to the mixture of fresh water draining from the land and salty seawater. As fresh water is less dense than saltwater, it floats above the seawater, and in some cases, a sharp boundary is created between the water masses, with fresh water floating on top and a wedge of saltwater on the bottom. ("What is an estuary?," National Oceanic and Atmospheric Administration)

ON THE DISCOVERY OF AN OWL PELLET BY A POET - An owl pellet is the mass of undigested parts of a bird's food that some bird species occasionally regurgitate. The contents of a bird's pellet depend on its diet, but can include the exoskeletons of insects, indigestible plant matter, bones, fur, feathers, bills, claws, and teeth (Wikipedia).

Final stanza, Genesis 2:23, The Creation of Man and Woman.

Jen Payne is inspired by those life moments that move us most — love and loss, joy and disappointment, milestones and turning points. She is the author of four books: *LOOK UP! Musings on the Nature of Mindfulness*, *Evidence of Flossing: What We Leave Behind*, *FLOSSING*, and *Waiting Out the Storm*. Installations of her poetry were featured in exhibitions at the Arts Council of Greater New Haven and the Kehler Liddell Gallery (New Haven), and her work has been published by *The Aurorean*, *Six Sentences*, the Story Circle Network, and WOW! Women on Writing; in the international anthology *Coffee Poems: Reflections on Life with Coffee*, the Guilford Poets Guild *20th Anniversary Anthology*, in *Waking Up to the Earth: Connecticut Poets in a Time of Global Climate Crisis*, a poetry anthology edited by Connecticut's Poet Laureate Margaret Gibson, and in *The Perch*, a publication by the Yale Program for Recovery & Community Health. You can read more of her work at www.randomactsofwriting.net or in her quarterly publication, *MANIFEST (zine)*.

Three Chairs
PUBLISHING™

Conversations in Print: Books, Art & More

Waiting Out the Storm
Jennifer A. Payne
44 pages, 5.5 x 8.5
$16.00, plus tax + shipping

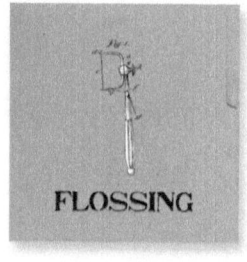

FLOSSING
Photographs by Jennifer A. Payne
54 pages, 6.5 x 6.5, Paperback
$14.99 plus tax + shipping

**Evidence Of Flossing:
What We Leave Behind**
Jennifer A. Payne
180 pages, 5.5 x 8.5, Color Photos
$21.99, plus tax + shipping

**Look Up! Musings on
the Nature of Mindfulness**
Jennifer A. Payne
288 pages, 5×7, Color Photos
$24.95, plus tax + shipping

Three Chairs Publishing
P.O. Box 453 • Branford, CT 06405
www.3chairspublishing.com

www.ingramcontent.com/pod-product-compliance
Lightning Source LLC
Chambersburg PA
CBHW030500010526
44118CB00011B/1022